FURLOUGH

FURLOUGH

By: Andrew Van Ella

Copyright © 2012, Andrew Van Ella

All rights reserved. No part of this book may be reproduced, stored, or transmitted by any means—whether auditory, graphic, mechanical, or electronic—without written permission of both publisher and author, except in the case of brief excerpts used in critical articles and reviews. Unauthorized reproduction of any part of this work is illegal and is punishable by law.

ISBN 978-1-105-64063-6

For Chris, who brought me a plant- you told me to let it grow just like my dreams.

For Mom, your strength helped my feet move when they were paralyzed by life.

Cover Designed by Brian Koppi

www.furloughbook.com

FORWARD

What sits upon the following pages is not meant to be analyzed; nor is it the reader's job to attempt to figure out what I was thinking or of whom I was thinking. This is not intended to be read like a novel cover to cover. My vision of the prose and poetry in FURLOUGH is similar to how we listen or appreciate music. It's a place to find solace in the words that you can relate to. Not all of the writings will be relatable but the ones that are should make you feel less alone in times of darkness. I began writing my junior year in high school as an escape from the confusion that life brings to all of us. I remember the feeling of relief and insight I could gain from unloading my words onto a clean white sheet of paper. Poetry allowed me to be free with my words and my form. I didn't have to answer to the constraints of traditional writing. Over the years I left that single sheet of paper for journals. There were months I would write furiously and then weeks of drought. I have used these to document my life and try to understand myself. In January of 2012 my mom began cancer treatment in Houston for a period of time. It was then that I collected what I thought was the most meaningful of my writings and began to put them into the book. There is much that never made it in and perhaps wasn't very good or even legible. Yet what has made it in comes from a place that many people don't know about me or themselves.

-Andrew Van Ella

1997

Then it happened. The slow spiraling motion toward all that is searched for. The journey was over and he was on its final leg- headed home. A gossamer shield of love stood before his weary war torn eyes; he reached to feel her between his finger tips and shuttered with every caress. He longed for her taste- finally it was real… as their lips met a sensation flowed throughout the travelers loins- taming every unloved bone in his body. She tasted like the first warm breeze of spring – fresh and new yet this breeze had made this path a hundred times before and stills seems virginal. The journey was complete-

Years of searching and almost deathly sorrow was worth this one embrace.

10.23.97

Why do I yearn for her so?
Is it that her lips calm my senses
Or because of the way her hands caress my soul?
The sad truth is that I long for her
And she doesn't appear
I search endlessly in my dreams
And I find is truth
When I search for a lost love…
I dig deep into myself and come up with fingers full of sand
The sand slowly falls through my fingers onto a forgotten
Shore
Where every grain will be lost at sea
I'm lost with her arms
Around my willing body
Her scent…
Fresh and warming

12.7.97

Everyone remembers their first…
A picture later seen through faded glass
Viewing a first after experiencing many
Remembering the entrance
                The penetration, an invasion
Slowly going from wet to dry
                Leaping in deeper and deeper
Until soaked,   completely
Your hands clinch to withstand the temperature of what lies around
                You
Grasping and engulfing your frame
        Frantic movement proceeds
Up and down over and over
Faster
Until you reach your goal
                Soaked and tired
You emerge victorious from its walls
Glance download at what you have finished
Everyone remembers their first…
        Snow   Angel

12.11.97

That tainted love- The only word I know…
        Without definition
Love   such an abstract concept
An unknown destination is where it rests
Many embark on an inward journey in search
Stepping onto the circuitous path which tells you one simple fact
Many choose to attempt for its peak yet few come out
        Completely   alive
I choose to hold myself tight
A sieve shows weakness
        If none come in
    Then none leave
        I am a force of immune love
Constantly imbedding laws to live by- I don't need her because I have
        Myself
This is my pain- a hellish lie told to myself
But faith never runs thin
     My realization is that I will soon run into true beauty- it will strangle
Me,   without warning
It will ambush my senses and leave me in the warm- delivery me from this
        Cold

1.30.98

Neatly diced tears
Lie before me upon
My internal cutting board-

I wonder if hers are
Sliced as neatly as mine

2.16.98

Pocket full of dark
The warm black
I hold tight
A bleak warmth
My summer sole
Days of light expose
My cream colored loins
Yet its opposite
Hides me in her shadows
Protected and stroked
In her nest
Settled comfortably inside her
Yes- I long for the
Lying back- admiring her
Starlit eyes
Their softness almost melts
Out and drips upon my eager tongue
I devour its essence
And pass
My time
      In open- toed shoes

3.2.98

They tell me it's good for me,
But her creamy brown foam
That slick milky surface that bites at my senseless tongue
A hair astray
        Lies of over Pete Rose
Raised glasses pay homage towards the STATE
        Weighted wings of none remembered memories
Headphones of the smooth center pore
        Chief-o'-stay-away-from-the-peak
But don't forget to sample a mirror twice
Jazz in New York
Reminds me of the duke- the vanguard
Last Thursday night, "she"
Lies only thirty miles
        It rolls further away- not like most ordinary things
I must make thought instead of think
An old looper
        A crevasse of a lost feather
And the butt of a Marlboro's dreadlock
Metallic green Volkswagon
A transfusion of us lost in the seas of blue numbers and you
Biting- tearing upon your senseless seams and
        Salivating over your miss and losing your HIT.
Oh, who am I to run from my steak and potato libation
        Thus I sit- left leg in rhythm
                A large fluidless glass of drought

2.26.98

Youth for a moment
The soft wrinkled
Sphere like device, if you will
Her fuel tank of white and
Nozzle to the new life we brought here together-
The ever changing from
Sweat and moistly tender
  To naughty and hard
Just as am I-
And when I speak of her twins she just
Curls into a little ball
And becomes young
  Again-
Cringes and smiles
  Only to be wrinkled once more-

1998

Dry
It's not that the rain has stopped
I've just gained a wrap of immunity

No longer
Am I porous
A sieve shows weakness
A place for the wetness to seek refuge
Not in these bones
It's cool tingling grasp
Once embedded itself beneath my skin
A virginal feel
One that almost replaced sleep
With energy
Sadness with hope and cold with warmth
But this soon dries until I find myself without the
Sensation
        Dry again
Its
        Lost in the air that evaporated
              you

5.17.98

Caressing your end
Walking back into the dark
Drinking the water that drowned
Your soul
Biting into that which caused
You to choke-
I now lay with my former death
Who attempts to breed new life
I fight and rip my innards with
Conflicting thoughts
Tear my lips
a w a y
yet I find her essence…always
trying to beat her yet I beat myself
strung and drip dried
drunk and seeing double
no sight is passed my way
I'm led on blindly
questioning
       biting my bottom lip just as she
bit me apart so long ago
forgiving the unforgivable
touching the culprit

       loving her

1998

Blind voice
A near collision
Leaves my senses cautious
A harmful timid kidnaps my body
My heart drips with need
As herself vehicle brushes past
A new scent occupies her
I long for the old…
My life arc's
Long and cold
Seasons change as does she
I dial her and I only receive a
Busy signal
Her voice is only a distant noise
From behind almost unrecognizable
Yet I don't change
I act the same and the lane narrows
Closing
In slowly on
My essence
Caught between the curbs of life
Only to be saved by your
        Presence-

1998

Hanged
I function hung over-
Over   you
Lies are what enter my body
Through my liquid dinners
Without us
She
                The bottle that attempts to satisfy my cravings
The fluid misconception that will never
Be you
                That which leaves me torn and hurting when I awake
Is no different from you
        I awake alone these days
Aimless attempts at hopes conception
Engulf me
Submerged in my emotional libations
I drown
            Alone and wide awake
Flaying demon settle
Wreaking havoc on my innards
Ripping the whole out of my being
All in lieu of her
Now
Glancing down at the floor I notice how different the view- without
My feet on the ground

5.17.98

Drip dried
These droplets of you…
Drain out only to become
A slow long think pour
One which itches at my palm
And dances as it leaps from my finger
Tip- in defiance it seems
        As if to say,   I'm almost
Gone-
This is a choice of no retreat
        Winter is upon us again
The taste of the pond is now a
Frozen barrier between me and my past
        Oh these selfish pleas-
Only the wind behind her drops of
Soon evaporated loss
The last wet grasps my nail
For the paused moment
        Only to pass with the same
Speed as the others-

14

1998

The soft caress of loneliness
A body of nothing lies beside
The small arch of her back hangs on my finger tip
Her taste... my greatest delicacy is lost
The secure warmth which will never be tangible again
I can smell her reminisce on my pillow
Feel her power in my soul
Plagued by mistakes
Weathered with regret
I long for forgiveness
She hears yet refuses to listen
My once fluid words
Are now only
        Fragments
And her smooth touch shattered-

1998

A subtle reminder of its smooth sleek lines
The gentle power harnessed inside her
A soft craving where I place myself
Consumed inside her- hanging on by my finger tips

1998

I just stood in the moment as long as possible
My stomach warm and my thoughts pure
The time that usually passes by
Stood beside me to admire her fluid motions
Each long leg and confident step sealed my grip

5.24.99

      An attempt to move forward
Without a feel-
      I recline smoking my love
Hungry addiction
      Run my fingers through my
Jet lagged heart
      I see the accused through
One way glass- I feel a need
To in•ter•ro•gate her feeling and handcuff
Her being
      The truth slowly trickles towards
The lights as she ashes her lost
Faith… in me
      When the verdict is in
And the case is closed
I question the justice of
A lost love

2.14.01

To hold a lost love is a love never lost.

     I stared with amazement at the beauty I could see within her eyes. It still knocked me to my knees- the chiseled nose, deep hopeless smile and the longing for something bigger than both of us. Yet all of my attempts went unseen. For her I was just a past memory; to me she was still that intangible dream. For a few long awaited hours we saw the happiness which we would never forget. She left me clean and calm. Though our goodbye was so unclear-

When will I see you again she asked. I want that moment back- I would have never left. My love which has endured is only mine and I see now that she may never love again with such innocence and clarity. For so long I would wonder of her. I've now made the trip, I've held her and to do this has made me new again. This love story has no ending only until I see her again will I be whole- even without her piece our puzzle is complete.

2.14.01

My Jaded Love
Sits in this- my glass of forgotten memories
    Wait...see through a door where people pass
The wait will never be too Long- As this heart will
Beats forever in hers
    This man whose ego
Crushed mountains will still cry
With visions of her smell
And sight of hope, faith, the forgotten future.

2.15.01

    This state of numb long's for tomorrow- awake cold again…alone next to the Body of who knows- she believes in the crooked eyes of the love liar

    My fear only sends her
Deeper
The abyss of this lost child, immature boy never to
Be a man-
Apart/together all is no
Feeling- my skin awakes not with a pinch but with the scent of she who's unchanged by time- nature is paralyzed against her beauty.

2.15.01

This rich leather exterior
Hides the broken life of potential- he still lives by names, $ and the worst
sense of human touch- Sparked by the thought
alive only again in the Kodak moment and
lost in tangible form.

2.15.01

Her armor defends
my bullshit-
    The armies of men seek
Her and the one solider
Bleeds on the battlefield of
Life-
    Sword in hand- shield lost
In the masses- she has passed
Yet her scent still lingers-
My death is for loving-
My life is for loving

2.15.01

Tripped up by the previous

Lost boys-

    Men Whose Hearts Beat Only in their Mind- whispering the word which flanked their onslaught.

I come unarmed, hopeless and searching to hold the grail- lost for so long…

Yet in the study, preparation and knowledge I'm powerless-

Vodka makes me weak, clock turns with ease- the fog settles and she enters this dreamlike drunken life- mumbled words lost in the fucked dimness of NY and lesbian roommates. I fumble for my gun and I realize no sidearm; she has got me again to slumber in the down pillow nightmare-

2.20.01

> The faucet of woman is pouring over this mobile life…
>> Laying, lying to/with

The secure and longing for

Voice from the dream- hearing

From the toy.

> My tripod of vagina-

So very different look, smell, motive-

I must concede to the love I have worked for- this is the risk

And the safe play wrapped into a beautiful package. Sex, love, friend all is one- yet I complain always.

Incarcerated with her/she was loyal and assumed to be true.

3.8.01

I once walked on water to hold her close

Vulture's fed at my hate I left behind me-

Loving only a dream

Still residing in the past

I held no tangible object only my lost glimpse of love now holds my skin

Together. I turned to see my road back. This risk Left no easy exit. A leap

Of faith on an unfaithful she robbed me of the dignity which

Remained. Falling to my knees

I licked the dirt from my

Hands- tasting the earth which

Gave me a forum. Take me now, Let me see my father Again- let me hug my friend Chris, help my grandfather and I catch the big fish.

My job was not done and my pleas went not granted. Only

Answer of hope spilled

Over me. Son pick up yourself

And keep fighting, love will

Be your best friend and

Worst enemy. So choose wisely

Who you trust- make your

Mother sleep well.

8.9.01

What is left to give
This heart doesn't feel
As I once did
It beats differently
These days
Just to keep the blood
Flowing
The love is lost to
Time
The rush I've forgotten
And the reality
Of life is upon
Us now.

8.13.01

Glance above my cap
The life before eating-
False smiles, lost trust
The hole in my chest is
Torn.
Not a friendly face to be
Found. No gentle touch to
Embrace. Only me to
Keep searching.

8.13.01

Stomach…
Always playing toward the next
encounter-
She is so allusive to me
Like a cat and mouse game
I search by not searching
The brush by
I breathe her in
The delayed eyes
I make love to her retina
The pupil in me to
Learn of her-
The hunter
The huntress

8.15.01

I charged ahead
Passing her by and
Leaving chance in my wake-
Glancing in the rear view
Mirror I see the beauty
Standing, waiting, longing…
This one way street
Allows no way backwards
The grip of bare knuckles
And flooded hopes keep me starring at yellow
Lines and the flashing
Signs of life. Somehow
Along the rat race I weaken the pace. Leave the
Motor aside
I will use the power I possess
To move me forward

10.29.01

Staring into hazel
Depth-
Worn from life
And still she was a rock…
I worked the room
Paying homage as
I deliberated the
Jury
Spilling my heart into the air
Leaving nothing to chance
She looked sad-
Then lost youth between
Us was the only common denominator
She slept and at
Peace I saw not
What I should have
But what I needed

1.6.02

Tears of anger
The only ones
Produced here
This factory
Is bringing this
Town down
Where are the
Dollar signs
Ladies-
Fuck this life
The grass is
Greener over
There
Need to just
Lie down
Lights are getting
Dim—
Staying the night

1.17.03

Visions of orange
They shackled my…
Dreams-
I dream of good-
Yet pain is the
Prize fighter
Ever last gloves
Robes… just
I believe in
The destiny of
Lies

7.21.03

Searching…again-
Where does she stay
Vacant heart I am
Yet she will be occupied-
Inside and out-
      No room left sir
Neon light flickers
No assistance for this wreck
Alone again-

7.6.05

My hate is the game
This blood longs only for
Pain- familiar to me is
This joke- this lie I've
Truly become
        Hope fades with each
Passing sip- on after
Another I swallow their
Essence… what have I become/all
Which I ran from
Is catching me- heavy
Feet I can't out run
The demons much longer

7.8.05

Longing for solitude
Searching on a barren
Desert- not even an
Oasis appears…sunburnt
thirsty I go only
To my knees and devour
Sand- vulture's circle
Overhead awaiting my
Dehydrated bones- no
Meat to feed off only
The frail mess I've left
Behind-

8.2.05

Touch is all around
Me- yet the touch
I long for is no
Where to be found-
I wait, watch and
Yet she does not
Appear- instead I
Find hollow hearts of
Which pass the lonely
Night beside me- my
Rock is out there to
Be found-

8.29.06

The eyes hold the
Secret behind- she is
The peak so wanting the
Love she was robbed of.
It's her mystery that
Keeps me coming back- I
Roll westward still knowing
Less than what I started with
I have doubts but those
Fade with the thought of
Her caress- those eyes still
Haunt me.

9.8.06

Turn down the lights-
Brain needs a rest-
Heart needs to grow again
Love isn't dead you are-
Breathe, breath- baby
Its time; let's take it
Slow… maybe ease into things
A little- no need to rush-
Slow
Little one slow-

3.21.07

      Blue open arms direct
Us- my head creates
Again- life smells of
Earth- dirty my hands
With soil these days-
I reach over and
Place an old CD in the changer- Bear takes
In the mountain air and
We have a path now-
A direction at least
A prayer- and no destination

9.3.07

Breathe… the dragon
Awakes from its slumber
Inside of your soul-
      What awakes this
Beast? Sleep my
Friend- rest your
Weary head- tired,
Tired- torn and
Beaten- let me be
In peace. No more
Pain- dry her tears by
Not causing them. Let
Go… breathe and let
It not be fire.

10.29.07

Insides coming out
Blood seen only through
My eye sockets-
Tears of red-
Lines tell a story
Almost too hard to
Tell…sober
Ink is this map
Of memories blurred
By sex, booze and
The hatred of myself-
Raw, beaten and
Dry mouthed I still
Awake and live to
Avoid being broken again.

11.17.07

Shoulder shift weight
To the left. Cloudy
Eyes gaze and wonder
Brain and heart fight
Soul decides to enter
The ring of indecision
Legs tighten stiff
Stomach rolls into itself
Fingers create a fist without
Moving-
Numb…threat dries
Breathe- inhale
I now begin to
Unravel and exhale

2.6.08

Side's change- we leave ourselves for others only to return to those we love.
Upon our return there is a vacancy-
The room is occupied and their heart is unwilling to let our lies in- we search for a pillow to rest our head…
We find whatever fabric caresses this weary soul. Along the way the cheap hotel
Scars our being-

2.27.08

She finds me in my sleep.
She kisses my lips and
Caresses my guilt ridden
Heart. I can feel her
Walls as they engulf my
Hard being. I watch
Her bathe as she used
To so often. I remember
Her eyes slowly changing
From heart to head. The
Barrier she had to put
Up to fight the storm
Which eroded her faith.

3.7.08

Chest is hurting me
Lately, not feeling as strong as the once young prize
Fighter used to. My voice
Is a bit raspier, my face holds the scars of my
Past. My hands are sore and tired from carrying the burden so very long.
Cough and bleed- get this
Sick out of me.

4.24.08

      Your cheek bones illuminate
By being- it is an upheaval
Of those dreamlike internal days
That rest in my soul. I
Believe in you… I believe
That we believe in one another-
Our knees touch unseen by
The on looks… we laugh;
Your cheeks that kill me begin
To strain
Yet the kiss was not had, we
Both went back and slept
Beside other people. Yet I
Doubt we were ever apart.

4.29.08

    Gentle- sadness surrounds all that we possess. Its long days of no hopes arrival- we used to have something to long for… we have now had that and it's not what was anticipated. The small Closet odor is filled with pain and lost memories of things we began yet never saw through. Bridges blown up; not burned. .The blue pill makes us sleep and dream of ghosts.

7.15.08

My blood cough finds
Her weary need- we turn
Together as one- no
Cue needed. I dry
Heave words with no questions
A course headed for a
Storm; she becomes the compass-
My bearing in a sea which
I the captain can no longer
Navigate

8.6.08

      Inspiration finds me in
My fragile state- loneliness and
Cold empty fill my vacant heart-
I long to feel sane again- I
Feel and hit my head on reality.
I dream of bleeding from my
Face, no towel will soak up the
Flood of hurt that rushes from
My pores. Yet again she seems like
An answer- a profit; I search to
Fill the lake that is already filled
By many-

3.10.09

Days pass differently now… there is a cloud of regret that follows my actions; the man that once was has now been broken down; Ruins remain- It will take a master mason to rebuild this ancient city. A former sacker of cities has now sacked himself. Raped and pillaged its own soul and left poor and longing for love left behind.

3.11.09

The ring is gone…
Our union sold to pay
Our circle of love and trust
Passed off to the next
Unlucky soul who walks
That tight rope
There is not much more that
Remains of her
The scent has
Passed
Maybe
a few holes where pictures
once hung
but now I have fallen on silence
I wonder yet if it stays at that
No hand reaches for a body
      No longer

7.1.09

Beauty awaits my arrival

I ride this thirsty horse down a trail dusty with lack of love-

Each stone that creates a stumble

Every storm that slows the journey only seems to make our reunion more clear

We are not sure on an arrival- we may even be there already.

12.10.09

Emotions move across
The sand- a breeze
Blows and my mind
Wonders- it changes
As I change- A
Wrong turn I know
Is wrong- a rite
Choice marks for
A restful sleep- Bear
Lays still, fan moves
Clockwise- I lie
Writing alone-
My choice, not hers.

4.6.10

I recall some of
Their smells, I can still feel the softness
Of the skin along
My finger tip- A
Few make me sick;
Yet I was the sickest
Of all- as I walk
Back- open closed
Door- seeing the larger
Window
I am finally in the room- I am present-

12.22.10

I know now that temporary
Fix is a lie- thus my
Hope fades and my darkness
Increases- I become a shadow
Of my old likeness- I am
A bruised body whose veins
Are filled with booze and pain
I share no light and shall
Forever live amongst the
Hellish world I've created in
This head- I have one
Enemy these days

1.13.11

We found each other through tragedy; yes- I see this now. It was the drive that never occurred. The smile and the future green grass; sunshine that we never had- so many songs, day's and star filled nights I would dream of her joining me on our journey home. Our whole life in front of us- I can still feel her hand- I can also see her fading smile and lost eyes.

4.27.11

I bleed differently these
Days- the joy drips
From my veins to the
Hollow ground below my
Useless feet- feet
Without purpose that walk only upon hearts
Of those who attempted
To love. Failed
I have and blamed
Their defeat on them
Yet the loss was won
Before we even met-
Dry cleaned

7.1.11

I glide back down
To earth- memory sweeps
Past my open porch- A
Glimmer of hope does stand
Ahead- purpose to be found
And love to be had- all
That has passed prepares me
for the waking moment of
judgement that stands upon
the sea of RED. Go see
the ocean; kiss the mountains-
feel the sand and taste the
salt. Let it burn your open
sore.

7.5.11

Breeze opens the screen
Door- let it in…
I lay upon my down
Throne and smell the salt
Breeze that finds a way
Through the needle size holes-
My pain is cured- my wound
Healed and memories forgotten

7.6.11

She rests alone
Tonight- I sit here and
Lay beside my thoughts-
No calm to find and
No body to cushion my
Fall-

7.13.11

The pen top doesn't
Click… I guess it
Never really did- Headed to
NYC to connect with a ship
That has already sailed- her
Bow is cracked- Iceberg
I guess. I phoned an ex
Who fell a sleep- I presume
It was important
Spent a morning doing tests
On my motor- didn't know
I needed to be raped- Its
My metaphor and my vehicle
I passed and posted a
Sticker that said so.

8.1.11

The bomb of flowers
Sticks upon the sheets
And down comforter- I never
Walked her downstairs; I planned
It so many times in my head-
She became a memory on this trek
I lost sight of her meaning-
The grail became just a
Cup- she said my
Kiss had become better yet
My unstable worse

8.4.11

Darkness and the silver
Screen- it was not you beside
Me as I wished it were- not sure I would be able to focus
Eyes and mind be on
The prize… you- I can still
Smell you- Ivory soap from
1994
Now I smell the new
You-
The reels roll and the curtain closes- credits

8.10.11

Sun drenched- no more
Shall I fake the sun
I see myself again- or
At least pieces- I attempt
To piece the puzzle; SHE
Is back again- helps me
Write- I sleep dreaming
And breathing fresh air- I
See the purple sky

8.28.11

I sit at a corner café
Await my libation-
Cool breeze walks over the small of the lake- sun attempts
To show her smile yet the clouds choose to rule today
A young German boy works the table- I order a beer – craving wine but
Strangely their only red is from California.

9.3.11

Home- yet came
Home to shit- comments
The one whom kills a mans
Hard on- the kind that
Steals your soul- those
Whom witches are made of-

10.3.11

Sumer ends again
The season of dying
Begins- I know that smell
It used to mean something
To me- there was a hope
Amongst that burnt leaf and apple cinnamon scent-
Yet I know it too
Well- there is only pain
Beyond the wall and
Sadness nests among their orchards.

10.08.11

Salted tears ring
Through the voice
Box-
My stomach is full
Bile and pain-
I awake to the dry to heave- nothing comes
Out because I have
Nothing left
      How to get the
Fight back
Boxer of not

10.20.11

Grey room with
A curved view of
A grey lack of- coupled with
The rolling hallways of doped
Out teenagers with no music
Hero's- pressure of blood running
Way too high- she tries to make
Excuses- I
Believe the charm gets in
The way a bit- In his
Head he runs through
Locked doors with
Chase- behind
Tables flipped and tears of rage
Meet the damp outside air
Of Lake Michigan

11.9.11

She will show herself
Tomorrow
      Silver tube over the great
Plains
Riding a clouded horse gliding
Toward the blue
I smell her already
The bomb- filled with
Prairie flowers
      Sun drenched days and the oak tree that
Becomes our umbrella

11.19.11

She sits upon my
Mind- I can feel the skin
And smell the flower- longing
For the next trip-
The hand hold, the embrace-
She glides back into my
Arms as she always did- on
Top she pitches a tent and
Camps- hair drapes upon my
Veil- I take in the smell

12.1.11

I found you in AUGUST
I love you in August- I
Kissed your dead forehead in the
Room white and plastic- your
Smell now lies upon me- I
Use your forehead now for
More than kisses

12.21.11

      Tortured man sits alone
She has passed many times
Grasp of pain says she must
Leave again- tortured
Man sits alone.

Dad, The Beginning.

www.ingramcontent.com/pod-product-compliance
Lightning Source LLC
Chambersburg PA
CBHW032134090426
42743CB00007B/591